Goodnight RED RAIDERS™

Written by Tiffany Roberts Kristynik
Illustrated by Matt Gardner

AMP&RSAND, INC.

Chicago • New Orleans

The indicia in this book are registered trademarks of
Texas Tech University® and are used under license.

Illustrations do not represent any specific individual
and any resemblance to actual persons is purely coincidental.

Goodnight Red Raiders™ is part of the Goodnight Team Series
and is published in cooperation with Morgan McDaniel, LLC.

www.goodnightteam.com

ISBN 978-099056038-8

Design: David Robson

Published by
AMPERSAND, INC.
1050 North State Street
Chicago, Illinois 60610

203 Finland Place
New Orleans, Louisiana 70131
www.ampersandworks.com

Published and produced in the U.S.A.
Printed in U.S.A.

1st Edition

Special thanks to the following, who allowed use of their images for reference:
Zackary Brame, High Riders Organization, Steve Massengale,
Neshadha Perera, Andy Reine and Texas Tech Communications

To request a personalized copy
or to schedule a book signing/school reading, email
Goodnightredraiders@gmail.com

Dedicated to Klayton and Klein
Mommy is proud of your Red Raider spirit

In memory of Grandma Rayburn
Thank you for being my biggest fan

To my Red Raider Family and Friends
Thank you for your support

The prettiest sunset skies are in the West Texas Plains

Where the wild wind blows and it rarely rains

Lubbock, Texas is quite the sight

When Red Raider fans yell, "Wreck 'em" and "Fight, Raiders, Fight!"

Every Red Raider gives a Guns Up® and smiles

While walking through Raider Alley and Raidergate for miles

As young ones lie down and say goodnight

Let dreams of becoming a Red Raider take flight

Goodnight Will Rogers and Soapsuds wrapped up tight

Goodnight Victory Bells ringing through the night

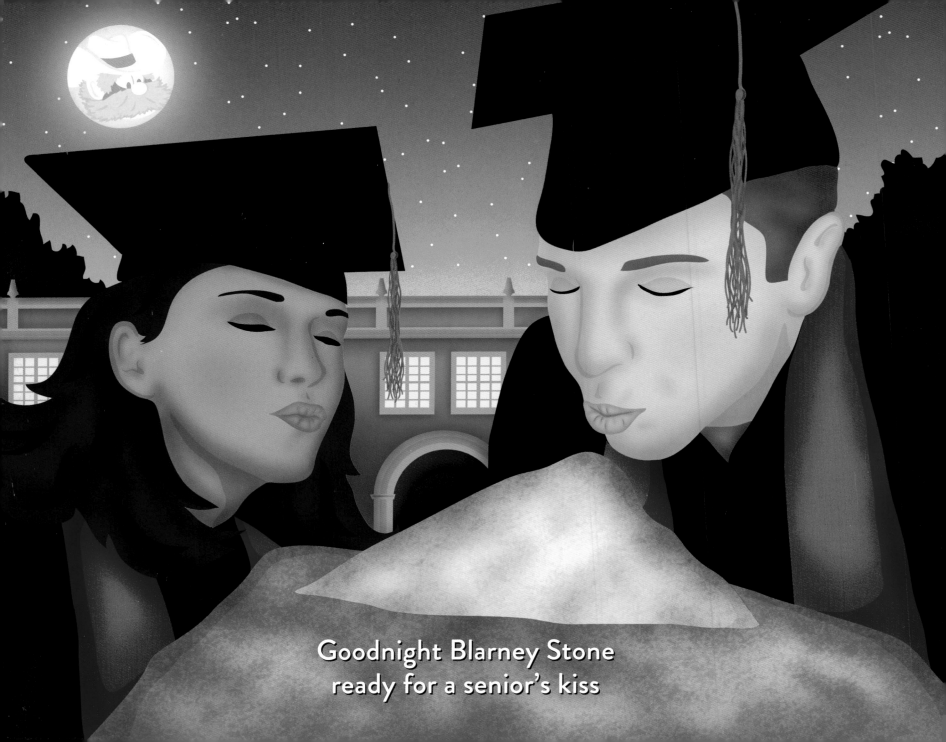

Goodnight Blarney Stone
ready for a senior's kiss

Goodnight University Fountain and Texas Tech Seal
where students make a wish

Goodnight basketball arena and titles clinched

Goodnight upperclassmen on the Double T Bench

Goodnight Dan Law Field and the pitcher on the mound

Goodnight Carillon bells and your beautiful sound

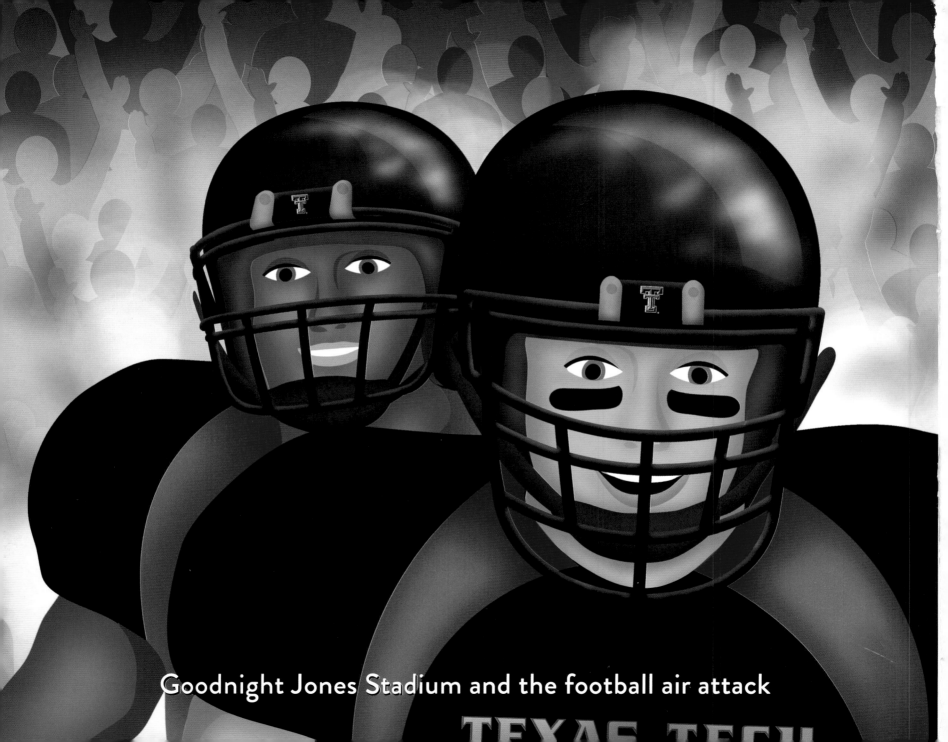

Goodnight Jones Stadium and the football air attack

Goodnight Matadors wearing scarlet and black

Goodnight Masked Rider and your horse storming the field

Goodnight Raider Red, whose identity is sealed

Goodnight Banging Bertha, Goodnight Saddle Tramps

Goodnight High Riders cheering Lady Raider champs

Goodnight Goin' Band from Raiderland,®
marching in formation

Goodnight Pom Squad and cheerleaders, yelling "Raider Power" with elation

Goodnight Double T class rings that alumni wear proudly

Goodnight to all Red Raiders® shouting, "Strive for Honor" loudly

Goodnight Carol of Lights on a chilly night in December

Goodnight Memorial Circle and heroes remembered

Goodnight Texas Tech,™ no other can compare

Goodnight Red Raiders™ and fans everywhere

GUNS UP GLOSSARY

Texas Tech University® TTU, founded in 1923, is a public research University in Lubbock, Texas. It offers over 150 courses of study and hosts 60 research centers and institutes. It is known for high research activity as well as its beautiful campus.

Air Attack The Texas Tech™ football team is fast and scores lots of points. The team is known for pass play offense, sometimes with no huddle, and drives down the field quickly, earning the nickname air attack.

Banging Bertha The bell is carried on a trailer by the Saddle Tramps and is a familiar sound at spirited football games.

Blarney Stone Any senior who kisses the stone is granted the gift of eloquent speech! The Blarney Stone was found by a group of engineers in 1939 and sits on a stand in front of the old Electrical Engineering Building.

Carillon Bells The 36 bells in the west tower of the Administration Building were a gift from Ruth Baird Larabee in 1973 in honor of her parents. The bells play beautiful music at celebrations such as the Carol of Lights.

Carol of Lights Twenty-five thousand red, white, and orange lights adorn 13 buildings on campus for the Holiday season. Traditional carols are sung by choirs to kick off the lighting event.

Dan Law Field at Rip Griffin Park is home to Red Raider baseball. In 1988, the stadium revived the name Dan Law Field after Mr. Law made a donation to renovate the current stadium. In 2011, the name changed again to include Rip Griffin Park.

Double T Bench Donated by the class of 1931, the Double T Bench sits in the Administration courtyard. Only upperclassmen are allowed to rest on the Bench.

Double T Class Ring The tradition started in the 1950s, but the ring was not made official for Alumni until 1999. Students wear it proudly with the inscription, "Strive for Honor."

Goin' Band from Raiderland® so named because the band was the first to travel to an away game. It started in 1925 with only 21 members; now there are over 400. The Goin' Band performs at home and away games, and special events. Its traditional "run-on" style adds excitement and anticipation to the performance and hurries one of the largest college bands onto the field.

Guns Up® A newer tradition, Guns Up® came from the Dipple family as a response to "Hook 'em Horns" of the University of Texas. Raider Red and his guns inspired the hand sign and it caught on with the cheerleaders and Saddle Tramps.

High Riders In 1976, the all-female High Riders came into existence as an answer to the Saddle Tramps. They support Lady Raiders™ athletics, attend home sporting events, and ring the Victory Bells after a win. Along with other spirit organizations, they play a vital role in supporting TT's Lady Raiders.™

Jones Stadium In 1947 the stadium, named in honor of Tech president Clifford B. Jones, was open for football games. It has undergone many renovations and in 2000 was renamed Jones SBC Stadium. In 2006, it became Jones AT&T Stadium, one of the rowdiest, offering an extreme home field advantage.

Lady Raiders™ term used to recognize the TTU women's basketball team.

Masked Rider The Masked Rider was TT's original mascot. It all started as a dare. "Ghost Riders" would circle the football field quickly and ride off so no one would know their identity. In 1954, Joe Kirk Fulton became the first Masked Rider. With a Guns Up® while storming the field, the Masked Rider is one of the most sensational moments at Tech games today.

Matadors The Spanish Renaissance architecture on campus is so beautiful and remarkable that it influenced the team name. In 1925, the wife of head coach, E. Y. Freeland, suggested the name and it remained until 1936.

Memorial Circle A place of calm, quiet remembrance and a beautiful memorial to veterans and students who have passed. The fountains and sidewalks provide a serene and respectable place for students to pay tribute to lives lost.

Pom Squad An elite dance team that entertains the crowd and cheers on the Red Raiders™ at home football games and many other sporting events.

Raider Alley Fans of all ages gather for tailgating in Raider Alley. The fun begins hours before game time and includes live entertainment, food and beverages, putting Raider fans in the game day spirit long before kick-off.

Raidergate Hosted by the Student Government Association, the official student tailgating section opens four hours before game time and gathers a crowd of up to 10,000 people.

Red Raiders™ The nickname claimed by students and fans of Texas Tech University,® replacing the original Matadors. It happened after a sports reporter used the term "Red Raiders™" while commenting on the strong season and red uniforms of the TT Matadors. Red Raiders™ reflects Spanish heritage and was officially adopted in 1936.

Raider Red Jim Gaspard, a Saddle Tramp, created the lovable caricature of TT's second mascot, Raider Red. He represents Texas Tech™ wherever live animals, such as the Masked Rider's horse, are not allowed. Cartoonist Dirk West drew the gun toting character who makes appearances in the Tech community. His identity is never known to the public. Only a member of the Saddle Tramps or High Riders may serve as Raider Red.

Saddle Tramps In 1936, an all-male spirit group that supports men's athletic events, especially football games, was formed. Tramps wrap Will Rogers and Soapsuds on game day. They begin games with a bell circle and keep the crowd rowdy with the ringing of Banging Bertha. Tramps also ring the victory bells in the bell tower, and select Raider Red. The long-standing group has extensive knowledge of the campus and athletics.

Strive for Honor This phrase from the Matador Song is etched into class rings to remind alumni of the academic excellence pursued during their careers at Texas Tech.™

University Fountain and Texas Tech™ **Seal** At the main entrance to the campus, these beautiful fountains form a gorgeous backdrop for the Texas Tech™ Seal, which was approved in 1953. Four symbols adorn the Seal: the lamp (school), the key (home), the book (church), and the star (state). The eagle represents country and cotton bolls, the region's primary cash crop.

Victory Bells Given as a gift from the 1936 class, Victory Bells ring out the most beautiful sound heard on campus. Two bells stand in the east tower of the Administration Building, one large and one small. They weigh 1,200 pounds. Ringing lasts for 30 minutes. They can only be rung by a member of the High Riders or Saddle Tramps to signify a Texas Tech™ victory!

West Texas Plains Located north of Caprock, the northwest panhandle region of Texas is flat, arid and often windy. The land area encompasses Lubbock, Texas and is sometimes called *Llano Estacado*.

Will Rogers and Soapsuds One of the most popular statues on campus is Will Rogers and his beloved horse, Soapsuds. Legend has it that the horse's rear end points to the rival Aggies in College Station. Saddle Tramps wrap the statue in red crepe paper before every home game. It is wrapped in black paper after tragedies or times of mourning.

Wreck 'em Taken from the TT Fight Song, this popular phrase passes from one Red Raider to another to provide a spirit boost among fans.

Matador Song

Written by Harry Lemaire and R.C. Marshall

Fight, Matadors, for Tech!
Songs of love we'll sing to thee,
Bear our banners far and wide.
Ever to be our pride,
Fearless champions ever be.
Stand on heights of victory.
Strive for honor evermore.
Long live the Matadors!

Fight Raiders Fight

Written by Carroll McMath

Fight, Raiders, Fight! Fight, Raiders, Fight!
Fight for the school we love so dearly.
You'll hit 'em high, you'll hit 'em low.
You'll push the ball across the goal,
Tech, Fight! Fight!
We'll praise your name, boost you to fame.
Fight for the Scarlet and Black.
You will hit 'em, you will wreck 'em.
Hit 'em, Wreck 'em, Texas Tech!
And the Victory Bells will ring out.